Advance Praise for Paul Yamazaki's
Reading the Room: A Bookseller's Tale

Colson Whitehead, author of *The Underground Railroad,* *Harlem Shuffle,* **and** *Crook Manifesto*:

All booksellers are the unsung heroes of American literature, but Paul Yamazaki is a superhero. With his unerring eye for the eclectic, the outsider, and the excellent, he has championed generations of writers. Because of his fearless and uncompromising taste, City Lights has become a cultural beacon whose influence extends far beyond its mind-blowing store in San Francisco.

Tommy Orange, author of *There There* **and** *Wandering Stars*:

The incredible story of one of the greatest booksellers to ever live. Told in a question and answer format, this book reads so well but also makes you feel you are in the room with Paul, listening to him tell stories about his life. Like Yamazaki, I come from a non-traditional background as a reader. City Lights was a refuge and lightning rod for me as a bookstore, and Paul is a crucial part of that storied place which will always hold a place in my heart—and now Paul and his book will as well. But it is more than a book about a book devotee, who has helped shape the publishing industry in the most interesting ways, it is a book about what makes us love to read, what ideas and styles draw us to books, it is a book about the life of an extraordinary man, and about life itself. Paul Yamazaki is a national treasure, and it was a pleasure to read this book the whole way through.

Rebecca Solnit, author of *Recollections of My Non-existence* and *A Field Guide to Getting Lost*:
If you love a bookstore it's whether you know it or not because you love a book buyer, a practitioner of that unsung art of choosing what the store will carry, a mixer of the cocktails on offer, a diplomatic negotiator between publishers publishing and readers reading, a curator of what is worth your attention––and in the book world no book buyer is more legendary than Paul Yamazaki of City Lights. He has made the job into an art, an ethic, an adventure, and not infrequently an insurrectionary act and half a century on retains his enthusiasm for the next great book. In this wonderful series of conversations he lays out his personal history, how he came to his role (via prison), what he learned, how bookstores work, what publications have most exhilarated him, why he thinks of himself as "a cross between a mule and a glacier," and the many friendships that came from his job.

Hua Hsu, author of *Stay True: A Memoir*:
A wry, stirring, profoundly uplifting ode to bookselling—complete with riffs on capitalism, San Francisco, jazz, even the meaning of life—from one of the underappreciated literary titans of our time.

Katie Kitamura, author of *Intimacies* and *A Separation*:
Paul Yamazaki is one of the greatest and most influential readers in the world. To hear him talk about books and the business of books is a mind blowing delight; this volume gives readers everywhere that opportunity. It reminds us that reading is an act of imagination, defiance, optimism and love. Paul brings the whole of his being to the world of books. May we all learn to do the same.

Hari Kunzru, author of *Red Pill* and *White Tears*:
There's a famous sign in the basement of City Lights that says: "I am the door." Paul Yamazaki has been the door for generations of readers and writers. He's a portal, not just into a world of books, but into a way of thinking about culture, of human communication and community. We're lucky to have him.

Eliot Weinberger, author of *An Elemental Thing* and *The Life of Tu Fu*:
This transcript of a two-day conversation with Paul Yamazaki is the *Tao of Bookselling*. One comes to the book expecting shoptalk, and finds instead a vision of the bookstore as a spiritual, intellectual, and political microcosm of the universe. How many of us are as wise as Paul about what we do, and can see the world in it?

Karen Tei Yamashita, author of *I Hotel* and *Tropic of Orange*:
Step into City Lights, corner of Columbus and Jack Kerouac Alley in North Beach, San Francisco, and you might not notice the curl of stairs that leads to a loft above what used to be the cash register. That's the cubby of Paul Yamazaki, professional reader, the guy who chooses, from 50,000 titles a year, the books that become the bookstore. If you catch Paul, invite him to Vesuvio next door for a meditation over drinks, the best way to get him to do his raconteur riff, a jazz rendition on what he calls "the possibility of joy," spinning stories, revealing his imagination of books in conversation. All this is hidden to most of us who wander in just to browse. But browsing is everything, and curating that space—its magic, possibility, and freedom, is Paul's unique gift and genius.

I love this little book…It's a love story to books and City Lights.

Preti Taneja, author of *We That Are Young* and *Aftermath*:

Reading the Room is a book that elevates, refreshes and restores my faith in words: it makes me excited again at the potential of being a writer. I am profoundly grateful that this book exists in the world, that its author is a bookseller, that he drinks whisky with writers in a bar across the street, and that his deep generosity and wisdom, that have changed so many lives and quietly shaped resisted mainstream culture while shaping something truly radical for decades, are now contained here. This book is a gem, and one I will return to again and again.

Aleksandar Hemon, author of *The World and All That It Holds* and *The Lazarus Project*:

Paul Yamazaki is a poet and a philosopher of bookselling, on top of being a fabulous storyteller. If you want to know why buying and selling books is far more than transactional or why City Lights is possibly the greatest American bookstore, you can find your answer in *Reading the Room*.

Vanessa Martini, Green Apple Books:

To know Paul is to know that he's a man of many words, many ideas, but few pretensions—so few that it can be difficult to get him to admit to his own genius. *Reading the Room* is a precious artifact that functions as a rare transmission from a truly great mind. Buying is perhaps the aspect of bookselling that the public encounters the most but thinks about the least, and to hear Paul speak about his methods and how he arrived at them is a genuine pleasure. If you're a bookseller, pull up a chair awhile and learn from the master; if you're a reader, know you'll walk away from *Reading the Room* with an entirely new appreciation for your local independent. Either way, what a joy!

Mitchell Kaplan, Books & Books:

Paul's commitment to the very deep waters of our literary life has made a difference, a profound difference. That Paul came to bookselling as a way to get an early release from a prison sentence rendered because of his activism is legendary...His championing and passion for new and diverse voices and for small and independent presses set an early example for booksellers everywhere. He demonstrated that these voices and presses would find their readers when given a chance. He continues to be a catalyst for change, a transformational change, that we witness today and every single laydown Tuesday...He's a friend and a mentor to young and old.

Melinda Powers, Bookshop Santa Cruz:

Reading the Room distills one thousand gin-soaked nights with Paul into a single energizing shot of a book that captures all of the passion, curiosity, and brilliance that he has taken from his life experiences and brought to City Lights and to the craft of bookselling. This little gem is all Paul—pure joy.

Stephen Sparks, Point Reyes Books

Paul Yamazaki, one of the most generous and genuinely curious people I have ever had the good fortune of spending time with, has given us a gift with *Reading the Room*. In this characteristically unpretentious and generous volume, a great bookseller has opened wide the doors to what it means to sell, write, and read books in the 21st century. It's a gift.

Jeff Deutsch, Seminary Co-op Bookstores:

Paul Yamazaki has raised up generations of booksellers. He teaches by example, including the lesson that discernment and commitment need not compromise kindness and generosity. In Paul's peaceable kingdom, engagement, listening, and curiosity are the marks of greatness, and enthusiasm the work. We are lucky to live in the time of Yamazaki.

Stéphanie d'Hubert, Seminary Co-op Bookstores:
This book demystifies the aura of what makes great bookstores and great booksellers. It goes deep to the core: individual and communal joy, curiosity, and enthusiasm.

Ode Books is a publishing partnership between the Seminary Co-op Bookstores and Matthew Engelke, Professor of Religion and Director of the Institute for Religion, Culture, and Public Life at Columbia University and Co-Publisher of Prickly Paradigm Press.

As the country's first not-for-profit bookstore whose mission is the bookstore itself, the Seminary Co-op Bookstores illuminates the profound cultural value of bookselling, in turn encouraging stakeholders of all sorts to challenge accepted practices within the industry and in adjacent spheres. With its focus on the browsing experience, the store cultivates an inventory which encourages curiosity and discovery.

Under the guidance of the Seminary Co-op Bookstores and Engelke, Ode Books celebrates book spaces and the book industry, publishing reflections on the cultural value of the book, analyses of the industry's challenges, and ruminations on the intellectual, emotional, and aesthetic pleasures of reading. Linking all of Ode's publishing is a celebration of the engaged, thoughtful reader who takes seriously the importance of spaces devoted solely to books.

Ode Books acknowledges these contributions to the production of this volume:

Designer, Jacket and Interior: Daniel Murphy
Cover Design: Erica Deutsch
Cover Image: Mark Shigenaga, Emiko Omori
Editorial Support: Vanessa Martini, Sam Gee
Marketing Support: Stacey Lewis, Marina Malazoniya,
    Kirsten Benjamin

Ode Books

Publishers: Jeff Deutsch and Matthew Engelke
Editorial Director: Noor Shawaf
Marketing Director: Clancey D'Isa
Editorial Assistants: Chloé Faux, Connor Martini

Reading the Room

Reading the Room

A Bookseller's Tale

Paul Yamazaki

A collaboration between
the Seminary Co-op Bookstores
and Prickly Paradigm Press
Chicago

© 2024 by Paul Yamazaki
Foreword by Rick Simonson

Published by Ode Books
5751 S. Woodlawn Avenue, Chicago 60637

www.odebooks.com

Permission of the publisher must be obtained prior to use or
reproduction of any part of this book. Requests for permission to reproduce material from this work should be sent to
ode@semcoop.com.

ISBN: 9781958846698 (paper)
ISBN: 9781958846803 (e-book)

Library of Congress Control Number: 2024930940

Printed in the United States of America on acid-free paper.

Table of Contents

Preface

The Seminary Co-op Bookstores' Ode Books is honored to present this slim volume as a distillation of the genius of Paul Yamazaki, beloved bookseller, City Lights Bookstore's steward and chief buyer, trusted arbiter and enthusiast. Paul has dedicated his care and attention to not only discovering and championing the books we must read, but to building relationships based on mutuality, curiosity, and literary nourishment.

Seminary Co-op booksellers and friends have held a number of conversations with Paul throughout the past two years, in the intoxicating stacks of City Lights, perambulating the streets of San Francisco, and over whiskey tumblers deep into the night. With Paul we've edited them into the format of one day and night's passage, collected to convey the essence of his wisdom, his passion for bookselling, and his life of letters, including the story of his tenure with the great City Lights, as well as to share the joy that it is to spend time in his presence.

This is the inaugural publication for Ode, an imprint of the Seminary Co-op Bookstores in partnership with Prickly Paradigm Press, established to explore various aspects of book spaces and the book industry, and to publish ruminations on the intellectual, emotional, and aesthetic pleasures of reading.

In every aspect of his life, Paul has celebrated communion among people who love books. For more than half a century, he's been among the most influential and beloved booksellers in America. Please join us as we hear Paul's story and celebrate the seventieth anniversary of City Lights.

Foreword

Reading the Room is a book, *the* book if there is to be such a book, to read if you have worked, presently work, or might work in a bookstore in the U.S., or really a bookstore anywhere. It's a book for anyone who works with books, writes them, publishes them, reads them—perhaps you who may be holding this in your hand. How do we see books, know, present, carry them; the single book, the many books; as parts of lists, as parts of seasons, their display, their substance; our current moment, the moments of years worked, lived, learned by; the curiosity and discernment offered and invited. These things, and more, are here.

What part do bookstores play and how do they do so? The aesthetic, editorial, and curatorial vision that Paul Yamazaki speaks from is strong and touches everything. Anyone walking into City Lights Bookstore will see that. But so is the 'business sense,' this being the economic system we're in, to keep that vision financially viable against the many forces that come at independent bookstores now and in decades past.

The stories Paul Yamazaki tells here—it's utterly vital that they are *stories*, orally transcribed stories, at that (praise for how well it's done)—make for shop-talk of a most profound kind. I count myself as lucky to have been part of or present for many of the stories, the late-night walks in one city or another, sitting in bars, talk of some of the most serious stuff, but also gossip and some of the book-nerdiest talk: backlist reordering, ISBN prefixes, who and what kinds of skill backgrounds do you look for when you're putting together a literary non-profit board. We've gotten lost, taken chance turns. Who got us *here*? However we've lost our way, we have always seemed to find something we wouldn't have found or known otherwise. Comical, all of it.

As well and long as I've known Paul—forty years and counting—this book holds many surprises. Which we still have to talk about. The Boy Scouts! This book *is* Paul on the page, his candor, and all his delight and wonder. There are places where you can even hear his laugh.

The people who are in this book! The people he's worked with at City Lights, family, people otherwise from life along the way, other booksellers, writers. Paul knows and talks all dimensions of book publishing and its people: the large corporate houses, university presses, smaller independents, and their interrelatedness to bookstores. To know where we are and might go, it's instructive to know where we've been. Paul is a student of history—that is also evident here. If there is abundant laughter in these pages, there is also telltale seriousness.

Paul was particularly mindful, as a younger bookseller, of those who came before him and the times they were in. Even as a not-so-young bookseller, he still is.

On a New York visit in September, 2023, among those whom he saw was Drenka Willen, she the editor who has given us Calvino, Szymborska, Eco, Grass, and so many others in translation. Now in her 90s, she is still at it with acuity and passion. Paul's visit bordered on the courtly—a present brought, and all was gracious, good conversation. A few days later, Drenka would write a colleague something to the effect that 'best friends from the old days' had called on her.

And as an elder, he is engaged in helping foster the work of those younger and working now and in times to come. Along the way, he's pointed out who's generally been excluded owing to race and class, and has done much to alter that course of things and our understanding of them. Necessary stories and necessary knowing. I've often been in his wake, meeting, greeting, learning.

It's particularly instructive to see him reach out to the younger and newer arrivals among us. In turn, it's heartening to see these younger book people seek Paul out—his warmth, his openness, his regard, his knowing. In that exchange between generations,

Paul also does something we don't see very often in our culture, especially from older to younger: he truly welcomes, he blesses. Not in a pronounced, officious way, but in his seeing, listening, acknowledging. He helps validate, give people a fuller sense of belonging and their place in the scheme of things, even when that scheme of things could use some radical re-arranging. Paul welcomes that, too: the changes that need to come, and are coming; the part the younger booksellers and others are playing to make things more just, equitable, inclusive, and reflective of the real, larger world.

Two months after that visit with Drenka Willen, Paul was back in New York to receive the National Book Foundation's Literarian Award for lifetime achievement and service to the literary community— to all community, really. All kinds of booksellers and publishing people attended because of Paul, some paying for their own ticket, some the guests of gracious table hosts who were also applauding Paul. One of those present that night, coming across the hall to greet him, was Hannah Oliver Depp, of Loyalty Bookstores. She is both very much part of the dynamic, changing present and a herald of a better bookselling future. Up to Paul she went with a congratulatory embrace, then she told how there was a time she stepped into a room with a hundred other booksellers in it, with Paul the only other person of color there. He made straight-away for her, hugged and welcomed her. If that was their meeting, it would be but a beginning, as Hannah, Paul, Veronica Liu, and others have set about doing more to make American bookselling in its official organizing more diverse and inclusive.

As one of many fortunate enough to have known, worked, partaken of what one partakes of in many a drinking establishment, talked and walked with him in comradely ways over every hour of day and night and over many years, I can say the work I do and the life I live have been enhanced immeasurably by Paul's presence. He is the best company. Paul Yamazaki carries the immensity and humility of being human with an integrity, passion, purpose, and radiant spirit that is rare among us. Turn the page, you will see. This little book says a lot. *Salud!*

—Rick Simonson, Elliott Bay Book Company

Part I:
A Walk Through the Bookstore

What a joy it is to be here with you today at City Lights on this foggy Saturday in San Francisco. Walking in the front door, I feel like I instantly know where I am. How do you choose which books to put in the browser's line of sight, how to signal what the bookstore stands for?

When I walk into Three Lives in New York, or other stores in San Francisco like Green Arcade or Green Apple, or on the rare chance I get to go to Seminary Co-op in Chicago, my eye gravitates to two things: one, the thing that I'm not familiar with and, two, something I may be very familiar with but now see in a new context. It's all about developing a conversation between the books. When they're placed side by side, they talk to one another. Our goal when you walk in is to make sure that, right away, you see books you haven't seen in other spaces and you see books you know, in a slightly disorienting way. Right now I'm looking at Jane Jacobs, Lewis Mumford, and Mike Davis grouped together—what a great party to be invited to.

City Lights was founded here by Peter Martin and Lawrence Ferlinghetti as the country's first all-paperback bookstore, and it maintains a dedication to progressive politics and modern literature. Please describe this eccentric corner building in North Beach.

City Lights since its inception in 1953 has been at 261 Columbus Avenue, which is at the intersection of Columbus and Broadway in the northeast quadrant of San Francisco. City Lights is at the intersection of three distinct immigrant and migrant communities. To the south is the Chinese community; to the north, the Italian immigrants established a community. To the east was the international district which was a community of many types of itinerant professions, including seamen, theatrical performers, saloon keepers, prostitutes, and prospectors of all types. The cultural, class, and racial diversities of these communities contributed to the fact that there was a range of housing types at various levels of affordability in the neighborhood, which provided affordable rentals for writers and artists.

The other important institution that was close to City Lights was the San Francisco Art Institute, whose faculty and students were important contributors to the bohemian flavor of this part of San Francisco. Every building on the block between Broadway in the north and Pacific on the south burned to the ground during the 1906 earthquake. Our building, 261 Columbus, was one of the first buildings to be completed in the reconstruction. It's somewhat hyperbolic to say there isn't a right angle in the building, but it's metaphorically so. You're walking through the same doorways that legends like Allen Ginsberg and Diane di Prima walked through. There's a resonance here. Imagine this space in 1953: 350 square feet, filled with magazines and books and people.

You've expanded several times since then.

Yes, City Lights now takes up three floors. It feels bigger than it is. There is eighty feet of frontage with generous window displays; they provide the main rooms with glorious light. We have changed some things, but the feeling is the same. The ceilings are twenty feet high, with tight stairways and exposed brick walls. It's astounding that we haven't lost anyone to those staircases over the decades! Co-founder Peter Martin used to have an office at the top of the stairs. The lower level is a subterranean world, with alcoves and archways that make it feel like another century. At one point, that basement was an evangelical church. There's an iconic photo of Lawrence Ferlinghetti here in front of a 1920s sign from the church days: "I am the door."

Serendipitous psychedelia. Originally the ground floor was a travel agency run by two Italian brothers. The space that used to be a separate building next door was a topless barbershop.

What guides your curatorial decisions? You have to leave out so much.

Trying to explain that is one of the most difficult things. For a time, it was Lawrence's taste that dominated the curation. Lawrence was always clear on what he liked and disliked. He was an outspoken critic of the Language School of poets, in part from his own vision of poetics, but also because of his acrimony with the poet Jack Spicer. But he understood that that friction was an essential part of the conversation.

He encouraged our relationship with Small Press Distribution, especially in the 1980s and '90s. If SPD was one thing, it was the central distribution point for the Language School of poets. Now that Lawrence has died, younger booksellers here won't have the opportunity and privilege that I had to create the collection in a back-and-forth with his reading habits and interests. We're not trying to freeze City Lights in time. It's a dynamic process. Each bookseller investigates their own subjectivities and their own responses to the texts while still understanding the context of the institution, how we arrived at this point. For example, people are surprised by the fact that we don't carry most current bestsellers—we could sell many copies, but from our perspective, they are not consistent with our values.

Instead, you have Fred Moten's *In the Break: The Aesthetics of the Black Radical Tradition* on display.

Having been a bookseller for over fifty years, my faith in the reader is profound. Our role is to bring them to a new door, to a new room. We are trying to choose the best of what's out there. How do we arrive at the best? Reading and conversations with other readers, other booksellers. If a book comes into your hands and you find yourself moved by it, ask: *How did this find me?* Answers to that question will always be fruitful and will always make you a better bookseller, able to make more informed decisions. People presume from our fairly healthy selection of critical theory that we are a highly educated, deeply knowledgeable staff. I can testify that this is not the case. But we are curious.

How many titles do you consider in a given year?

At least 50,000. There is no way that we could encompass all of that. Even if we could, it wouldn't lead to a very interesting bookstore. I've been at state bookstores in Beijing, and they do that and it's fascinating. It's intimidating, but it leaves it up to the reader to navigate. What we do as booksellers is that we create an environment where there's a framework for that sort of navigation. I'm awestruck by buyers of bigger stores like Elliott Bay, which is nearly 20,000 square feet. I don't think I could buy for even a 5,000-square-foot store. I'm the finch that has such a big beak it can't fly. I can crack a nut, but I'm not good for anything else. I do like immersing myself in the world. I have an almost obsessive quest for excellence in detail and execution, and I look to people who put the time in for inspiration, whether it's Coltrane or Steph Curry. We all have different capacities. I'll never be able to shoot three pointers the way Steph does, or play *A Love Supreme* the way Coltrane does, but I can explore the limits of what *is* possible for me to accomplish.

What are the factors that go into the buying decisions you make?

For a buyer in a store, I think it's helpful trying to envision where a book will be in the store: how is it going to fit on your shelves? Will it be face out, spine out? Will you display one copy, five copies? How many linear feet do you have to fill in the particular area where it belongs? Our most conventional shelving is poetry—A to Z—but almost everything else is distinctive, not just in naming, but in how the books are in conversation with each other. Should we arrange it regionally, break continents down by country? There are many legitimate approaches. What we excel at is that we are able to have this shimmering conversation. You can only put in 33,000 titles. We carry 1.3 copies per title. Certainly, for me as a buyer, it is so easy to get into a backlist buying frenzy and make it very tight to shelve. That section is already at 120% capacity. My colleagues are ready to kill me because it takes them ten minutes to shelve two books.

And you have to be mindful of the browser's experience when the shelves are that tightly stocked.

Because there are so few face-outs, you have to be willing to explore, to invest time and curiosity, and hopefully you'll be able to come back and start to get a sense: when you see a colophon for a certain publisher, does that excite you? Is there a conversation happening in this section which intrigues you? You'll be able to create your own personal library in this bookstore that is forever changing. It will be part of a constantly shifting display. The surface of the ocean always looks the same. If you look at it closely, it's always changing.

Do you think in terms of what will help keep the store in business?

You develop an internal map of measurements. I like to compare what we do to pre-industrial navigators. We've always said, *I have a feeling about this, a feeling about that*, but now we're combining our micro-observations with a bit of empirical knowledge.

Now you can look at productivity per linear foot. You can actually think in a fiscally coherent way: look at books that sell one copy every twelve months and appreciate that as a fiscal contribution. We need to explore strategies for becoming fiscally sustainable while recognizing that the real goal is to guide our readers to a more expansive horizon. If you offer that portal, even if their initial impression might be that what you're recommending is arcane or dense or difficult, if your assessment of the book is accurate, you will find a reader—not just a reader, but a delighted reader.

You've also talked a lot about access.

Our challenge is to do this work in contexts where we haven't done it before: lower income communities or communities of color. I see brave and adventurous booksellers operate where our previous sense was that this isn't possible, but they're showing that it is. The worst thing we can do as booksellers is underestimate the reader. And the City Lights audience is interested in the literary and artistic avant-garde internationally. Lawrence understood that he didn't have to love something to understand that it was important. I learned from him to distinguish my own preferences from what we ought to make available in our bookstore: major streams of possibility and resistance.

What kinds of resistance?

I believe it's important to resist the capitalist impulse. As it developed, capitalism has taken away the ability to work as an individual within a group. Not so much resistance against a thing or an object, but resistance to the fact that capitalism with its atomizing motives has a low ceiling for joy. Whatever we end up calling it, the determining factor is: what is the possibility of joy? At the end of the day, that's what we're looking for. Current modes of thinking help suppress things that bring us joy. We think of independent bookstores as toolboxes to recover those things, to understand the ontological basis for joy for the individual. And from that develops mutual aid and cooperation. Mutual aid is not a binary thing. I think of it as more of an improvisational music group, intertwining traditions to create a better whole.

You've done incredible work over the years giving a broader reach to Black-owned presses.

Three key presses from a City Lights point of view were Africa World and Red Sea, Black Classic, and Third World Press. The books published or distributed by these organizations are critical to how City Lights represents the broad scope of American culture. At conferences, all three were literally in the basement—you could call it a "ghetto corner" of the book fair. It was the best part of the fair. The conversations that you could have with those individuals working the tables were great. The booksellers, agents, editors who were interested in what those presses were doing were always the most fun people to talk to. You would automatically have common ground and would hear about things you hadn't heard about before. It kills me that there are really good booksellers now who have never heard of those presses.

What is the responsibility of independent booksellers to promote a racially diverse selection?

City Lights believes very strongly that American culture and literature cannot be accurately represented if there is not deep BIPOC representation in the authors and subjects that are presented on the shelves of City Lights.

Over the decades there has been a barrier, coming even from independent booksellers who said Black authors' books didn't sell. The beginning of the breakthrough was Ta-Nehisi Coates. His book *Between the World and Me* did really well and opened a lot of eyes about the persistence and excellence of One World's work, in conjunction with the Penguin Random House sales reps. That helped in the process of turning things around. Hopefully people will investigate backlist and see what is possible in their communities. Our role as booksellers is to take readers to places they didn't expect to end up.

But you've made it clear independent bookstores can't do that on their own.

Right. Nor can Graywolf, nor PRH do that on their own. City Lights has been able to keep 40–50 % people of color on staff. And when a person comes into the store, they recognize themselves on the shelves, too. We don't have specific sections that say Black Literature, but a reader of color who spends time at City Lights will realize that we recognize writers and thinkers of color as part of the critical mainstream. There can't be a critical mainstream without them.

We do a disservice to readers if we don't do that.

There are larger things that will take time and a lot of thought to do, but there are things that we, as booksellers, can do now in selecting the books we stock and how we present those books. Being able to create the balance in the bookstore between what's essential and what can sell is such a critical thing. Certain titles may not sell that well because they've been around for a long time, but someone browsing philosophy who doesn't see Walter Benjamin or Cedric Robinson might not come back because they don't think the store is serious.

What about political diversity?

We do carry Schmitt and Hayek. We want to have an informed dialogue. We carry Russell Kirk. There was the Penguin *Conservative Reader* that Kirk edited and it's a really valuable book. For City Lights, Tucker Carlson is irrelevant. But if you expand that into literature, Céline is obviously, on a personal level, highly objectionable. It's also fucking good writing. Pound is a little bit more complex. There is a clear divide between what he expounded and what he wrote. Are we taking Pound off the shelf? I don't think so. It's not legitimate to remove that voice or channel from the discussion of poetics.

What about when it comes to bad behavior?

Often there seems to be a level of outrage that is not commensurate with the act. To me, that deadens the conversation. It seems almost more to be a demonstration of solidarity than real solidarity. For a bookseller, real solidarity is being able to state clearly why we carry this book or that book. We know significant writers who, as part of how they conducted their lives, would be criminally culpable. Am I taking that work off of the shelf? I believe we should not expect moral rectitude from our creatives. I would prefer everyone had high moral standards and treated people fairly and with justice. There are some people who are major assholes and major artists. There are living artists whom I would prefer not to spend any time around, but whose work we will continue to carry.

Have your own politics shifted over time?

No, not if you mean anti-capitalist. A political position is an ongoing project, just like there is a dialectical process to how we live, the things we take in, how we practice. There should be a continual evolution of those things. How we consider gender roles has evolved tremendously. Our definition of Asian-Americans has evolved dramatically. It has sometimes been a process to think about how those definitions have changed. But new is not always right. Across all political perspectives, one of the weaknesses of Americans in general is their ahistoricism. It's easy to deplore this or deplore that, and to advocate for something that is somewhat inaccurate or not as nuanced as it can be. Within communities of color, how we've defined ourselves in relationship with each other has changed a great deal. Younger activists have pushed us in a way that's really positive.

City Lights has taken notable risks in publishing, famously putting out Allen Ginsberg's *Howl* in 1956.

A poem like "Howl" puts complexity directly in our faces. It's hard to put ourselves back 67 years ago to see the level of courage that Allen had to write that poem and put himself out there. And for Lawrence to publish it and continue to publish it. It's still a challenging poem, all these years later. That's another case where Allen's behaviors weren't always perfect, by any standard, but it was something he owned. And we've never been looking for comfort, in my opinion. We're looking to make things more equitable. Justice and the fight for justice have never been comfortable. Those at the forefront of it have never been comfortable. The least we could do is challenge ourselves and question our assumptions, knowing we will make mistakes and be wrong at certain times. At some point people will see us as wrong, but it is up to us to defend our opinions. This may just be an old curmudgeonly bookseller speaking, but comfort is not how I define things.

Is that generative discomfort part of City Lights' legacy?

If we look at the streams of art and literature through the 300 years of the development of capitalism, our pushing back—what City Lights represents—is to challenge those notions of authority, to challenge those strictures. The artists who have brought points of vision and beacons of hope within a capitalist system have always been problematic. The challenge to the reader, then, is how to parse all of that? How to develop your standards of aesthetics and morality? I feel very strongly that those cannot be received; they must be developed.

Looking around the store, I wonder which books mean the most to you? Which ones do you go back to again and again?

A Man Without Qualities I've started at least two times, but I never got past 750 pages. The book I reread the most is *Moby Dick*. I would love to reread Karen Tei Yamashita's novel *I Hotel*. Karen is one of the most gifted writers of this century. She never approaches a story the same way, which is one of the reasons, I think, she's not better known. *I Hotel* is ten novellas, each approached in a different way and yet which still tell the story of a small group of Asian-American radicals in the late 1960s. Of really significant books written in the 21st century, I think it is one of the most underread.

Do you believe in rereading as a habit?

I don't know how many times I've listened to Coltrane's *A Love Supreme*, so I don't know why I wouldn't do that with books? But there is always new stuff. The demand of our trade is to help readers make a path. As purveyors, we are all trying to sell something. What's different about bookselling is that we are trying to guide people. For even the most serious and regular reader, sometimes they want guidance from us. Some of our bookselling friends are amazingly good at that: being able to take time with an individual reader and, in ten minutes, alter their lives by putting together a new reading program for them, open another channel for curiosity.

City Lights has had some incredible booksellers.

For a short period of time we had Philip Lamantia on staff. Philip was one of the most extraordinary conversationalists—it was as though Eliot Weinberger were working for us—both encyclopedic in knowledge and with an ability to express it. Philip always worked downstairs, never in fiction or poetry. You knew someone had seen Philip when they'd come up the stairs with a dazed but happy look on their face.

Why do you love *Moby Dick*?

It has such mythological proportions. It is deeply tied to American history, both in positive and negative ways. Fundamentally, it's such a wonderfully told story. It's so rich. Anyone trying to extract so-called meaning from it, I don't know, but it's just a great story. The old Arion edition is my favorite because there is material that shows the objects, places, creatures. John Evans, proprietor of Lemuria Books in Jackson, Mississippi, has a great collection of Melville. He also has a Beat section with a framed note from Lawrence.

Before we go and get ready for tonight's event, let's take a quick look at the books you have in your office.

Sure. What catches your eye?

Here's *The History of Philosophy* by Grayling. *Black Futures*. Darby English's *Among Others: Blackness at MoMA*. *On Earth We're Briefly Gorgeous*—I count three copies. *Bottom's Dream*, an unreadable book that went out of print the second it was published. Alberto Manguel's *Library at Night*. Two copies of *Latitudes of Longing*, one from Elliott Bay's Rick Simonson, the other brought back from India. On top of a stack, *Ferlinghetti's Greatest Poems*. The Library of America's collected Albert Murray. A gorgeous, gorgeous, gorgeous *Negrophobia: Urban Parable* by Darius James. What is it?

Like a cross between Terry Southern and Ishmael Reed. I had the good fortune of having lunch with Darius and he's as mad as his book.

First edition jazz books: Ornette Coleman, John Coltrane, Ross Russell...

Ross Russell's *Bird Lives!*, a biography of Charlie Parker published by Charterhouse—an independent press—is important. I bought that at Marcus Books, a key bookstore, and one of the longest running Black-owned bookstores, operated by Drs. Raye and Julian Richardson. Marcus continues to this day in Oakland, run by the family members. But when I bought this, it was just off Van Ness on McAllister Street. And if you were looking for something like Ross Russell or *Coltrane: A Biography* by Cuthbert Simpkins—the first biography of Coltrane—the only place you could find them was at Marcus. And because Julian Richardson was also a printer, they had posters of Coltrane and Eric Dolphy and people like that. But significantly for City Lights, Marcus was also, at that time, the only store in San Francisco that carried the Heinemann African Writers Series, which they introduced me to. And because of the Richardsons and Marcus Books, I was able to get those into City Lights. From there, two feet of books turned into a whole room of literature.

Who were other publishers that you would fill out the collection with in 1985?

There was a publisher run by this very eccentric fellow out in Colorado called Three Continents. And there were university presses, like Indiana, doing translations of Soviet literature as well as 20th-century Chinese literature. Penguin. People forget about Avon doing a significant amount of Latin American literature. Avon was not just García Márquez, but that whole generation, as well as Rushdie's *Midnight's Children*.

Speaking of which, here's a beautiful hardcover of *Midnight's Children* and *Satanic Verses* and *Moor's Last Sigh* and *Jaguar Smile*, all first

editions. A galley of *Wind-Up Bird Chronicle*. First editions of *Anywhere but Here* and *Secret History*. First editions of Cormac McCarthy, including *Blood Meridian*, which is almost impossible to find.

Scott Davis, my colleague of many decades, introduced me to the work of Cormac McCarthy. Scott insisted our customers read *The Orchard Keeper*, *Outer Dark*, and *Child of God*, so, of course, when *Blood Meridian* was published by Random House in 1985 we enthusiastically ordered a stack. The initial print run was so small. I think at first City Lights was the only independent bookseller that sold that book in double digits.

Wen Fong's books. Angela Davis's *Blues Legacies and Black Feminism*, which has all the lyrics right in there. *The Power of Black Music*. A couple of biographies of Monk, and of course two editions of Ashley Kahn's *A Love Supreme*. And then into history and more history, including Civil War histories and Hobsbawm. Nice hardcover of

The Age of Extremes. **Hugh Thomas's** *Conquest* **in hardcover.** *The Landmark Herodotus* **in hard-cover. A Compact OED, of course. No library is complete without one.**

Which, even with the magnifying glass, I cannot read anymore.

Letters of Beckett from 1929 to '40. That's fun. Complete Nathanael West. I've never seen this edition—talk about genre. I see James Ellroy there. Do you read much genre fiction?

Not as much as I would like to, but people like Chester Himes, Raymond Chandler, I think are essential. People have discovered in recent years Delany and Butler, which is immensely gratifying. I'm always disappointed that, whether it be Library of America or Everyman's, that there is not a unified edition of the Harlem Detective Series. *[Ed. note: As of this printing, the Everyman's Library has released a single-volume publication of* The Essential Harlem Detectives *by*

Chester Himes.] And in light of what Colson Whitehead has done, I was thinking that would be a great time to do such a volume.

A *Guide to Manhattan Booksellers*, an Avon book from 1979. That's fun, including where to get a Swahili book. Remainder bookstores has its own chapter. *Early African American Print Culture* published by University of Pennsylvania. And a bunch of manuscripts. An ARC of *White Teeth*. The complete works of Isaac Babel.

Babel's stories are so evocative and, at least in these translations, there is a simplicity of language without sacrificing any kind of narrative drive or characterization. And I do have great weaknesses for box sets, as you could probably tell.

A Secret Location on the Lower East Side.

If you ever find a copy of this, get it. This is essentially a history of post-war independent publishing.

Did you ever get involved in publishing yourself?

The short answer is no.

Why, do you think?

A good editor requires a deep sense of empathy, both to a writer's intent and to the potential of the text. An editor also needs a technical mastery of the English language and a good sense of structure. I do not possess *any* of these skills.

***Divine Days* by Leon Forrest is here in hardcover.**

Toni Morrison was his editor. One of my great frustrations over the years is that nobody has been responsive to the idea of the Toni Morrison Library. My idea was that Random House would recollect all the rights and that Toni would write a short introduction to each one of these volumes. I only had one occasion to spend any time with her at all, and it was one of my proudest moments. She bummed a cigarette off me. It

was at one of Sonny Mehta's dinners at ABA. Sonny
and I would sometimes go out and sneak a smoke, and
Toni joined us. Then Alexander McCall Smith joined
us. I'm standing there with Toni Morrison and Sonny
Mehta and Alexander McCall Smith, who has amazing
argyle socks and was a very entertaining fellow. And,
I mean, the pleasures of an inconsequential moment!
You leave yourself open to things and you just don't
know what's going to happen.

**On that note, let's see what might happen at your
talk tonight.**

Part II:
A Book Event Q&A

Here we are now in front of a packed house at City Lights celebrating you and your contributions, Paul. Your friends and fans are here and we're going to pelt you with questions. To start, please tell us how your family contributed to what you're doing now.

As I've thought of a bookseller's epistemology and my own personal journey as a bookseller, I've come to realize that some fundamental aspects of what I do as a bookseller are rooted in my upbringing and early childhood. I think curiosity is a fundamentally important tool of the bookseller. Booksellers are able to craft curiosity as a multifaceted tool that is particular to each bookseller and to each bookstore. For me, this multifaceted tool has developed slowly over decades and I continue to hone it. As I've thought about this subject of curiosity and the crafting of it into a tool, I have come to realize that the foundations of that curiosity are rooted in childhood. Even though I've resisted the thought of a biographical approach, it seems I have no recourse but to talk about aspects of my biography that have shaped this curiosity.

Good. You grew up in California, but your family was of Japanese descent and you were born in the Midwest, no?

I was born April 17, 1949, in Cincinnati, Ohio, because my dad James Nobuo Yamazaki was doing a residency there. But then we left Cincinnati in 1949 to go to Japan. My dad was originally scheduled to be working in Hiroshima, but the British wouldn't allow him residency because he was of Japanese descent.

And that's a grudge he carried with him for the rest of his life. Eventually they made him physician in charge in Nagasaki—the American zone of occupation—for the Atomic Bomb Casualty Commission for pediatric studies.

In 1951 my father and mother, James and Aki Yamazaki, returned to the United States after nearly two years in Nagasaki. My father had been conducting pediatric studies on the effects of the atomic bomb in Nagasaki with Japanese doctors who had survived the bombing there. It must be remembered that in 1951 we were less than six years removed from the dropping of the atomic bombs in Hiroshima and Nagasaki, in August of 1945. The West coast of the United States, and California in particular, had a long history of sanctioned and unsanctioned violence against people of color, particularly Black, Brown, and Indian, but certainly there had also been extreme violence against East Asian and South Asian people.

Shortly after our return to the United States, my parents attempted to buy a house in the San Fernando Valley, which is immediately adjacent to the city of

Los Angeles. The prospective seller of the house my parents wanted to purchase told them that despite the fact that he wanted to sell them the house, he couldn't. The neighbors had objected because my parents were perceived as not American because of their Japanese American heritage.

During the Second World War, my father had earned a bronze star and a purple heart in the 106th infantry division. He was captured at Battle of the Bulge and was a prisoner of war from December, 1944, to April, 1945. So, when he heard this about the house he wanted, he put on his uniform and knocked on every door on that block.

How did it turn out?

Well, let me start by saying that my dad was at the School of Medicine at UCLA, which was still in a very embryonic state in the early '50s. At that point he was thinking more in terms of an academic and research career and not as a practicing clinician and pediatrician. A colleague at UCLA said, "I know this house for sale in Van Nuys, and you're looking for a place. Wouldn't you like to buy it?" My dad said yes because the price was something he could afford. After coming to an agreement with the seller and then the seller backing out, his colleague came back and said, "Actually, people on the street say they don't want you there." My dad being my dad was really pissed off. He put his military uniform on, and he literally knocked on every door on the block and said, "I'm the guy who's going to buy that house. Do you have an issue with that?" Nobody would cop to having complained. So, he went back and shared this information with the seller who agreed to sell again, and he bought the house. But he never really liked being there, for understandable reasons, and he maintained a somewhat skeptical attitude towards neighborly courtesy. My mother got attached to the house and the neighborhood. But he never did. Plus, he was really busy. He opened a pediatric practice in the mid-'50s and drove about thirty thousand miles a year doing house calls; I went with him sometimes.

My parents were New Deal Democrats and supporters of Henry Wallace, Franklin Delano

Roosevelt's vice president, in the 1940 election for Roosevelt's third term. They were not enthusiastic about the election of Dwight Eisenhower, who defeated Adlai Stevenson in the 1952 presidential election.

They were especially concerned by the continued hostility to Japanese Americans returning to California after being incarcerated in concentration camps during the Second World War. Members of the family had been dispersed throughout the United States during the war and the years subsequent to the war. My mother was put into a camp when she was a senior at UCLA. She would have graduated that spring. She was one of the Japanese Americans who didn't receive a diploma until fifty years later.

Anti-communist crusades were being led by the Republicans, whose major mouthpiece was Joe McCarthy. The act of suppression of political and cultural dissidents in the post-Second World War United States led my parents to conclude that, for the time being, they would keep any political ideas in their back pocket. They did not change their progressive attitudes, but they chose not to talk about them much publicly. Instead, they focused on the academic success of their children.

And how did you do in school?

Terribly. Much to my parents' despair and frustration, from a very early age I demonstrated that academic success was a goal that I was not going to achieve. Despite their remedial interventions, nothing seemed to change. My report card stayed a flat line: a 2.0 from first grade through 12th.

What was your school like?

Huge. The high school and junior high school I went to had about 5,000 students; it was a six-year school from seventh through twelfth. There were no African American students. There were only a handful of Asians. The biggest minority group was probably Jewish. And so there was a class divide. Some emergent Chicano families were pushing their way into the middle class at that point. Those were the people my dad was closest to. They did manufacturing and light industrial work. The other part of the school was mostly Jewish, mostly professional, upper-middle class, and more politically liberal.

If you weren't into school, what was exciting to you as a young man in California in the 1950s?

One: the Los Angeles Dodgers. Two: the Boy Scouts. Three: the Ash Grove.

Okay, let's take those one by one. When did you first get into the Dodgers?

My father became a Brooklyn Dodgers fan when Jackie Robinson signed with them in 1947. He celebrated the victories of Althea Gibson, Floyd Patterson, and Muhammad Ali, dating back to when he was fighting as Cassius Clay. He critiqued Patterson, stating that he was too quiet. He liked how Muhammad Ali was vocal in his critique of race in

America. So, it was natural that the Dodgers would be my pick, too.

The Boy Scouts?

My father and his two brothers were Eagle Scouts, as were my older male cousins. In my father's point of view, my becoming a Boy Scout was as natural as the sun rising—it wasn't questioned. I was initially skeptical, but it was in Boy Scouts that I formed the initial tools of critical curiosity. They developed in me the ability to take the experience of walking through a landscape and then translating that to the two-dimensional realm of a map, and then being able to take a map and be able to create a mental image of the terrain that I would walk in the future with a great deal of accuracy.

There was a family, the Gilberts, who were the bedrock of the troop—it seemed to be a family endeavor. My recollection sixty years on is that they were a religious Christian family. Mr. Gilbert was the scout master. Mrs. Gilbert was very supportive and had a wry sense of humor. John Gilbert was the big, athletic son. Bev Gilbert was the daughter about a year or two younger than John and much like her mother, with a good sense of humor and really supportive of this scruffy set of Boy Scouts.

Mr. Gilbert, the scout master, was authoritative in a very even-handed way. He never raised his voice to us and was always instructive in teaching us camping techniques. My recollection is that during the Second World War he was a tail gunner in the Air Force. He survived 24 missions and then became a Los Angeles police detective.

One of Mr. Gilbert's tenets as a scout master was that he was responsible for us scouts mastering basic techniques, after which we'd have a lot of independence in the field. On long walks each scout would be allowed to set his own pace, and if a scout chose to walk by himself over the course of the day, that was perfectly fine as long as that scout hit the rally points on time.

Boy Scouts has been fundamental to my book-selling life because it was in Boy Scouts that I began to appreciate the differences between cultural background and cultural outlook, and to be able to define what success was on an individual basis and not according to societal norms. I'd hike alone sometimes and like it. Boy Scouts taught me independence, spatial awareness, and how to get from point A to point B. At one point we even hiked from Yosemite to Three Kings Canyon.

The map could give you a sense of elevation change and where the twists and turns of the trail were and how to determine where our rally points would be. There was a lot of freedom to determine how we were going to approach any four-to-six-mile stretch. I consider that spatial awareness a fundamental skill for a buyer at City Lights.

And finally, your third inspiration as a young man: what about Ash Grove?

Not too long before my sixteenth birthday, one day I was doing chores in the backyard. I was doing tours around the yard and had this black plastic AM/

FM radio plugged in with an extension cord. I was fiddling with the dial and landed on a FM station that was playing American roots music. The first complete track this DJ played was Paul Butterfield's "East-West." I had some superficial familiarity with the blues, but I'd never heard anything quite like this extended improvisation.

From this point on, every Saturday I would dial into this station and listen to this particular disc jockey. He gave me a comprehensive listening education of blues artists produced by Willie Dixon: Howlin' Wolf, Muddy Waters, Otis Spann, Sonny Boy Williamson, James Cotton, and many others.

As I listened to this program every Saturday, I would often hear the name the Ash Grove, where they would announce that somebody like Howlin' Wolf would be performing in the coming week. I would come to learn that the Ash Grove was owned by the Pearl Brothers, who I understood were from Brooklyn with very pronounced left leanings. I didn't understand anything about their politics, but I came to trust their programming! A wide variety of blues players played there, as well as musicians from other American roots traditions such as Doc Watson, Clarence Ashley, Clint Howard, and also performers from what I guess one would call neo-folk music, such as Ramblin' Jack Elliott and Barbara Dane. Another local band who performed there frequently was the Rising Sons, which featured Taj Mahal and Ry Cooder.

The same year I turned sixteen, I received a gift from my paternal grandfather: a 1954 Chevy Bel Air. I also found a job at AH Fong's restaurant, a Chinese restaurant for non-Chinese people. AH Fong's was owned by Benson Fong, an actor most well known for playing the number one son in the Charlie Chan film series. I worked Fridays and Saturday nights, and after my shift ended around 9:00 or 10:00, I would frequently leave the San Fernando Valley and drive over to West Hollywood where the Ash Grove was located.

For almost two years I did this and was privileged to see performances by Willie Dixon, Howlin' Wolf, Muddy Waters, Mississippi John Hurt, Sonny and Brownie, Doc Watson, Clarence Ashley, John

Hammond Junior, Jack Elliott, and the Chambers Brothers. The Ash Grove became the foundation of my musical explorations that continue to this day.

And when did you move to San Francisco?

In August of 1967—with very little intentionality. What a time to be an ignorant kid! There was probably never a better time to be an ignorant middle-class kid than that period. I'm walking down Haight Street in late summer of '67, wearing a yellow London Fog jacket, wingtip shoes, these whiskey brown slacks, and I'm going, *Wow, this is really different*. If you're male and eighteen or over, you had to decide about what you were going to do about Vietnam. If you were middle-class and in college, you took the easy way out and got a 2-S deferment. To me that seemed to be an unfair advantage. I come from this background of military service. The kids going to fight seemed very little different from me, apart from their economic status. So, I decided not to take a 2-S. I took my 1-A. My parents weren't very happy about this. But as I got swept up in the student Left, I saw that there were many different ways of resisting.

You wound up at San Francisco State. Why did you decide to go to college?

It was never questioned. We were a Japanese American family. I was dealing with the desire to assimilate, to play football and try to be part of the mainstream—with mixed results. I was an immensely indifferent student. I must have been memorably bad because Mr. Berkowitz, who I think was my tenth grade English teacher, he came into City Lights after I'd been working there for a number of years. And he was literally dumbfounded. He saw me working in this landmark bookstore, and he just could not fucking believe it. He said, "Yamazaki, you work in a bookstore—in *this* bookstore?"

And you happened to get to San Francisco in time for the Summer of Love.

Everything was happening so fast. Santana's playing in the park for free! Janis Joplin is playing in the park for free! Music was all over; politics was all over. I was getting accustomed to all these things and then starting to actively engage with other Asian Americans who weren't family members, who had different experiences and different outlooks, and participating in the antiwar movement. It was all a part of the educational process. Middle-class kids, of whatever background, were going through a conversion into: *I'm a fucking revolutionary, badass motherfucker*. I had not the fucking slightest clue what I was talking about. I see now that there was this hardcore, dedicated group of people who'd fought this uphill struggle for a long, long time and, all of a sudden, they're inundated by tens of thousands of ignorant kids like me. We swamped the organizations. We didn't know what the difference between a Trotskyist and the CPUSA. We didn't know the heroism of people who were doing voter registration. At San Francisco State, most of the students of color, particularly the African American students, were five, six years older, and they had so much life experience. Some of them had served in the military or been in SNCC. I was running into a lot of people who had really great depth of experience and was fortunate to learn from them. So, I was still relating to all this as a San Fernando Valley middle-class kid working in the student cafeteria.

What kind of organizations were around then?

The African American Students Union. Filipino Americans had their own organizations, as did Chinese Americans. Latinos, too. Some were based around cultural affiliations and some were based around class affiliations. Around the time that I got there, they were united under the banner of the Third World Liberation Front. Japanese Americans didn't have a separate organization, but a new organization had been organized out at Cal, the Asian American Political Alliance, AAPA, and that's what I became part of. We were the least experienced. None of us had real prior political experience. Nobody had been in the military. Nobody had done any of the voter registration work. Most of us were under twenty.

You could wander around and stumble into stuff. One day in Ghirardelli Square I was handed a leaflet by a young woman who I thought was very attractive. It was a benefit for the Black Panther Party, a screening of *The Battle of Algiers* at the Surf Theatre. I didn't know what the Battle of Algiers or the Black Panther Party were, but I knew I'd like to see that young woman again, so I went. She wasn't there, but I did see David Hilliard and Bobby Seale. I was more conservative than my parents—I even played football in high school—so it was an amazing experience to be there.

Lawrence Ferlinghetti, George Whitman, Nancy J. Peters, Robert Sharrard, Paul Yamazaki, and Richard Berman in front of City Lights Bookstore, February 1985. Courtesy of City Lights Booksellers and Publishers.

And when did you end up at City Lights?

I started working there in winter and spring of 1970, packing books on the publishing side. At the time I was excited about Amiri Baraka, Bob Kaufman, and Ted Joans. As renowned as he is, Lawrence Ferlinghetti still gets overlooked. His ability to bring in active working partners has created incredible consistency in the history of City Lights. For seventy years, it only had two directors: Nancy Peters and Elaine Katzenberger. If the bookstore has an aura, it's Lawrence who created that aura. There is an intentionality there, whether it's credited or not. His ability to collaborate in that sense is a large part of our sustainability.

Were you also enthusiastic about Allen Ginsberg?

I respected Allen a lot. He was incredibly smart and wise, and you could see he was such a positive influence. It's never been easy to be an outsider in this culture. But by the time I came to City Lights,

I thought he was over the hill as a poet. What distanced me from the Beats was politics, which were mostly white. Kerouac's relationship to jazz seemed very superficial. I was more excited about what was happening in Northern California. Al Young, Ishmael Reed, Nathaniel Mackey, bell hooks (Mackey's then-partner), Frank Chin, Jessica Hagedorn—I mean, holy shit! Of course I was interested!

Wasn't Ferlinghetti considered a Beat?

Lawrence never accepted being called a Beat himself. He respected all of the traditions, but thought it was only a partial element of resistance, and one part of a vision that persists through Western Literature through the last 250 years. He saw other major streams that he thought City Lights should be a part of. He always thought all these schools were way too restricted. It's not that he's turning his back on it at all, but the web of influences like Gary Snyder and Diane di Prima mustered come from so many different sources of influence. He was exploring the work of the Négritude movement. I, too, found Jayne Cortez interacting with Ornette Coleman much more interesting than how most of those post-Beat writers were into the rock and roll and punk thing. One of the things that distinguishes my role at City Lights is that I took my differences as a person of color and a critical communist to question the mainstream of bookselling at the time, and that allowed me to see how to make decisions to benefit all readers. When you look at a music section, it doesn't have to be Grateful Dead; it can be all sorts of other traditions.

Is it fair to call you an autodidact?

I'm one of the people inspired by 8th Street Bookshop and Cody's and City Lights and Kepler's. Many of us had been kicked out of school. Many of us had found the procedural parts of college not all that interesting and not tied to learning. We were drawn to bookstores because of the cultural things that were happening at that time and because of the expanse of independent bookstores.

The trio of stores in the Bay Area opened within 18 months of each other: City Lights, Cody's, Kepler's! KPFA started at the same time. You combine that with the dialogue that was happening with Robert Duncan and Kenneth Rexroth—there was so much ferment and that inspired so many of us when we got to learn about the history.

You mentioned 8th Street Bookshop. Could you talk about your initial connection to New York?

Ted Wilentz had long since retired but it was always an amazing thing to talk to him about what it was like to be a bookseller in Greenwich Village from the 1940s–'80s. All the St. Mark's people were former 8th Street booksellers. Jason Epstein always felt that so many of his publishing ideas came from wandering through the stacks of the shelves of 8th Street and seeing what was there and what was possible. Hence Torchbooks and hence Anchor Books. If I remember correctly, Jason was involved directly in both of those. That crowd was in the middle of the Village, along with the painting crew at the White Horse Tavern, Allen's crew, and the midlist authors scattered throughout the West Village. So many publishing people lived south of 23rd Street in those days. My first trip there was in the early to mid-'80s. I became a buyer in 1981 or '82 and was very inexperienced. I was peppering everyone with questions. My first visit to Random House was the only time I wore a tie. I thought, *I'm going to talk to André Schiffrin!* So, I found a tie someplace and it was probably deeply crumpled and very stained. It made me think of my father and how indifferent he was to how he dressed.

Tell me more. What was your father's family like?

His father came over in 1904 and was in San Francisco for the earthquake. But there was a bounty being offered to Asian Americans to leave San Francisco and go anywhere else. So, he took the money and came to Los Angeles. He became an Episcopal priest. His wife was an orphan and they were introduced by white

Christian missionaries. They were married here in San Francisco at Grace Cathedral.

Did they have children besides your father?

The eldest, John, also became an Episcopal priest. My dad was the next, and then a younger brother, Peter, and then a sister, Louise. John and Peter were Goldwater Republicans, and James and Louise were New Deal Democrats—and, even more extreme, they were Henry Wallace Democrats.

And your mother?

Akiko Hirashiki. They were Okinawans. Her parents came from around Naha. She was also born in Los Angeles and raised in Boyle Heights. Her father was a wholesale produce grocer and he came over in 1911. He was rounded up on December 8th, and before he wound up at the Camp Amache/Granada Relocation Center internment camp, he was kept in Texas. He spent over a year there before he was reunited with the family. Her brother also went to a camp. He was in one of the better camps, as with most of the teenagers, and he ended up enlisting in the army. He never went overseas because he was still really young, but he ended up as part of the occupation forces in Tokyo.

What was your mother like?

She was quiet. Very supportive, very artistic. That seemed to run in the family—her sister went to Juilliard for piano. She was interned for ten months at Manzanar.

How did she and your father meet?

They originally met at UCLA. Then when she got out of the camp in 1944, she went to meet her sister in New York. She and my dad had a weekend romance before he shipped out. They spent a few months together and got married, and she got pregnant. She had German measles and my older brother was born with a congenital heart condition, so he was dead within months. And at the same time, my dad was missing in action. He'd been captured at the Battle of the Bulge and become a prisoner of war. The war was pretty traumatic for her.

And for your father, too, I imagine.

He was assigned to a new division which was, just by coincidence, also the same division that Kurt Vonnegut, the writer, was in. So, if people want to know about his experience during the Battle of the Bulge, read the first fifty or sixty pages of *Slaughterhouse-Five*.

Finally, how did you meet your wife, Sara Chin?

She was working on an early PBS show called *Bean Sprouts*, geared at Asian American kids. A group of Asian American musicians threw a rent party we both went to. I was playing music when she walked in and I noticed her right away, but she left before I got a chance to talk to her. But I knew almost everyone at the party, so I was sure it wouldn't be too hard to see her again.

I asked everyone who she was, and no one knew who I was talking about. I thought I'd never find her, and then a few months later she walked into City Lights.

Did she buy anything?

The first book she bought from me was the Cuban writer Gabriel Infante's *Three Trapped Tigers*, the Harper edition. We got married in 1984. That Infante book still sits on my bookshelf.

Part III:
A Post-Event Bender

You very patiently answered our questions, and we're off to drink now. You're a drinking enthusiast. Why?

Drinking covers at least two major themes that I'd like to underline: generosity and dialogue. There is no more democratic place than a bar to ruminate with friends and colleagues. I don't know what there is about being at a good bar, but it levels the playing field. Everyone can have equal voice. Certainly, it's something that I learned from sitting down and talking with publishers, editors, and reps.

It's a joy to see you bond with people over books.

Any single book has a constellation of conversations, consequences, and causes. We feel enhanced by these conversations, both in specific and general ways. They always lead to something else. It seems that conversations about classic books just pick up from where they leave off, alongside books that have been published since. For publishing folks—editors in particular—a main reason they take time to talk to booksellers is not to promote their own books—although our comments are welcome, usually—but to learn about others' books. Old school publishers kept a bottle in the drawer. Business happened around conversation. Drinking was a sidebar to the conversation. New corporate offices don't lend themselves to that.

We're at a bar across the street from City Lights drinking whiskey. With the edge sloughed off, can we hear about some of the tougher stories from your career?

Well, I want to make sure I mention the late Francis Oka, a young Japanese American poet who was a few years older than me and for sure wiser. I was fortunate to have him as friend. For me, he's crucial. He was a natural leader in a quiet way. He was a Japanese American born in 1946 and he worked at City Lights from 1965 until 1970. He died in the winter of 1971 in a motorcycle accident at the age of twenty-four. He was co-editor with Janice Mirikitani of *AION*, one of the first Asian American literary journals that emerged in the 1960s. Francis was the individual who got me the job at City Lights.

I was incarcerated in the San Francisco county jail, and he told Lawrence Ferlinghetti, Shig Murao, and Robert McBride to hire me so I could get an early release from jail. (I was doing a few months for inciting a riot, illegal assembly, and an assault and battery thing—I hit someone who assaulted a woman I was with.) And they did hire me. I went straight from jail to bookselling.

I've seen pictures. You were always in a London

Fog jacket and khakis. Why was Francis so important to you, besides getting you hired?

He was so much more level-headed than I was. I was getting arrested a lot in those days and I had an unearned status as a rebel because of that. You're a bonehead and you're getting credit for being a bonehead. But Francis always kept stuff in perspective. He was engaged without being reckless. The "Days of Rage" bullshit infuriated me at the time. The Weathermen didn't help anything. They actually enabled law enforcement agencies to come down with more legal justifications or societal justifications than they would have, and my father had raised me to see a lot of LAPD policy and behavior as racist. But in my mind back then, I'm the second coming of Che Guevara. At that time the draft board was hot after me. I flipped them the bird, sent these insolent notes, finally received a 1-Y designation: psychologically and morally unfit for service.

I feel like the culture back then could be sort of macho. Is that fair to say?

Yes, and honestly Francis and I were complicit in undermining one of the women we worked with, Penny Nakatsu. The undercutting of women was so prevalent then. I'm ashamed now of our behavior as males. The sexism was so egregious. The women did so much of the work and yet were always relegated to the back door. They were asking a good question of the men in the movement: *If you're set on developing something better than the mainstream system, how could you replicate oppressive behavior?* That question was not resolved in any meaningful way for a very long time. Dating back to the '60s, many self-styled revolutionary males were extremely sexist, to put it mildly.

But you found kindred spirits. Could you talk about Rick Simonson?

The amazing reader and buyer at Elliott Bay Books. He is responsible for so many of the connections I've made. He is famous for walking into almost any place where books are part of the business, and the world seems to stop when Rick gets there. He has bridged continents and oceans. He is known as well in South Asia as he is here. He brings books in both directions. Those of us fortunate enough to call him our friend will have books whose American version is still a couple of years away from publication. Rick has an admirable, old-fashioned quality of being a writer of notes and letters. He's assiduous in his acknowledgement of galleys and things he finds of significance.

You and he share a talent for enthusiasm.

I don't know if we are particularly fortunate in the immediate time we're living in, but when we talk specifically about books and look at this last decade, I'm of the opinion as a professional reader and bookseller that this is one of the richest and most rewarding times to be a reader of literature. There does not seem to me to be a hegemony of any style or region, and so, for the most part, there hasn't been a looming presence like a Roth or Bellow or O'Connor. But I would make the argument that the period we're in now is as rich as the 1945–60 era.

Further reason for enthusiasm now, beyond the wealth of great books to read, is the wealth of young people coming into the business, including people of color, but really across the board. I am so curious and excited about the present. Despite all the challenges we have, I am excited about the possible futures of the book business. The intelligence and enthusiasm have always been there, but the discipline of the current generation of booksellers has foreknowledge about what they're getting into. It took me decades to get an understanding of what it meant to be a bookseller.

It even took decades for City Lights to carry hard-covers, right?

We began as paperback-only. In the early 1980s, City Lights was on the brink of going out of business. Only one wholesaler would sell to us. Initially we were very democratic about the whole buying process, and a publisher's rep would sit down with the whole staff, which was not really workable. Five booksellers sitting down looking at catalogs, none of us knowing really what we're doing, and the poor reps are I'm sure thinking, *Who are these clowns?* Plus, we had a really bad payment history. But Nancy Peters and Lawrence Ferlinghetti, to streamline the process, appointed me buyer. It had been a long frustration of mine as a reader—not just as a bookseller—not being able to read *The Bluest Eye* when it first got published, or *Song of Solomon*.

You mean because they were in hardcover first and that was prohibitively expensive?

It just wasn't within our reach as booksellers because we were a paperback-only store.

So even though you worked at City Lights, you were imagining yourself in the place of the reader?

Yes, and that was frustrating. I knew that Pantheon was publishing these incredible books, Edward Said and Michel Foucault, titles that we'd have to wait a year for them to come in. So many contemporary authors—Don

DeLillo, Paul Auster, Toni Morrison, Alice Walker—
were publishing new books in hardcover and we would
have to wait for the paperback publication a year later
to sell them! So, it really wasn't a bookselling decision,
it was a reader's decision. We wanted to replicate what
publishing was doing, breaking new ground and being
very adventurous. To be wedded to paperbacks at that
time meant we were not able to shape reading culture
in the same way that publishing was doing.

**Would you say it was, in a way, a selfish decision
to do this?**

Oh, absolutely, no doubt! But then as a buyer you have
the ability to always be making selfish decisions.

**So how did you decide that this was a selfish
decision worth pursuing?**

Oh, the advantage of when you're nearly out of business is you can't make a wrong decision. If you make a
fortunate decision and rescue the operation, great, but

we were going out of business. Everyone on staff who remained had resumes out to other bookstores, every one of us. All of us applied to Cody's, all of us applied to Moe's. I did some post-mortem forensics on this. What we were able to determine was that, at the point when we made these changes and I became buyer, two-thirds of our annual income at that time was equal to our unpaid bills that were over 180 days old.

Oh my God.

Oh my God is right. Every publisher cut us off.

The buying process had been very democratic. You were all sitting with the reps. Was the decision to bring in hardcovers also democratic?

No, that was unilateral and without consultation.

Did you just place an order and wait for the books to come in, or did you tell people what was happening in advance?

The way I recall it, I didn't consult with anybody, and I didn't inform anybody until the books came in. The impact was immediate. Sales increased dramatically. I don't know this for a fact, but I've always surmised it was an accountant whom I never met who said, *Whoever's doing this, let them continue.* Because it was immediately noticeable. The level of excitement, first of all, with the staff: *My God, hardcovers!* And things that we were interested in reading. It was also clearly apparent to people who came in and browsed the store.

Now we have systems where we can watch sales pretty much as they happen, but back then there were still paper ledgers, I'm assuming?

We figured it out by working on the floor. And then surmising that somebody upstairs was noticing. You had no way to tabulate sales like we have today, so there was nobody at City Lights who thought in those terms, including myself. I still guess it was the accountants hired to do our taxes yearly who noted to Lawrence and Nancy just how dramatically sales had changed.

And what was the reaction on the floor once these previously unknown hardcovers started showing up on shelves?

People were excited. Great readers like Scott Davis and Bob Sharrard were on the staff at that point. They were excited to see these books that we've been wanting to represent. Before that there was an ego thing: *You're a bookseller and you're behind the curve?*

I've always found it really admirable that you're buyer for *City Lights*. It's not the Paul Yamazaki bookstore; it's still City Lights. You've been able to balance your own personal taste as a reader with what serves the store best.

I always characterize myself as a cross between a mule and a glacier, and neither one of those are too self-reflective. It's not that I don't question myself, but I guess in a general sense, I'm very self-confident. I think the important question here is the relationship with the reps. Very clearly from their point of view, before, we did not know what the fuck we were doing, and they were really amazingly generous. They tried to provide a structure, to help me understand how to do my job. If I'm thought to be generous to people emerging in the business, it starts there.

How do you mean about the reps being generous?

It started with—and this is how different the business was from today—Lawrence Ferlinghetti, Nancy Peters, and Richard Berman, who was the manager at the time, writing a letter to everybody that we owed money to, which was *everybody*, a really long list. Dozens of letters. Without exception, everybody worked with us. They put credit ceilings on us. Our deal with Random House, for example, our credit limit was $2,000, which even then in '80s dollars was an incredibly low ceiling for trying to do frontlist and backlist. But we were able to stick to our payment program. And, time and again, people were being really generous about increasing the ceiling, but it took us over two years to dig ourselves out of that hole.

And what about the reaction from the public? Besides the buying of books reflected in the sales, do you there was a shift of attitude in how you were perceived by the reading public, in terms of what kind of a place it was?

I think reading culture is still very oral, but even more so then, because there was no such thing as social media. But word got out really quickly. We didn't make any public announcements about any of that; just like it's always been, the books are there. The intention behind City Lights from its founding was to make it comfortable for browsers. In Lawrence and Shig's mind the purchase was always secondary, at best! Browsing lets the reader become critically self-aware of their own needs. If they need help from us as booksellers, we can give it, but it's their choice. We are better at doing that now than we were then, and it's always been City Lights' primary ethos.

Would you say that carrying those hardcovers served as a signal immediately that this was a

serious bookstore?

Yes. I think it changed the perception of many readers
at that time, who really wanted to support City Lights
and would have preferred to buy a new hardcover from
us rather than Cody's or Printers Inc. The recognition
of the fact that we had those titles, and a wide representation of authors of color, and university presses,
too, was just immediately noticeable.

**How did you get to the point where you said, *I'm
asking this question of how this book I love got into
my hands, so to answer that I'm going to go to New
York and visit some editors in their offices?***

Well, there again it starts with the reps. For Random
House when it was just Random House, what made
the Random House sales group on the West Coast
incredibly unusual was a rep named Maggie Castanon:
one of the first women reps working for a trade house,
and one of the first people of color working for a trade
house, and also, as far as I could tell, one of the first

actively nursing mothers to go to sales conferences. I couldn't even call myself a bookseller at that point. I'm just a reader working in a bookstore. Maggie's coming in to talk to the manager. At that time, we had a two-minute conversation. Couldn't have been much more than two weeks later, I get addressed to me personally a copy of Edward Said's *Orientalism*. In that short conversation, Maggie was able to grok me: *I've got this exact book for this exact kid.*

Was that a book you had heard about at all before that point?

Orientalism continues to this day to be a foundational work for me, and, I believe, for the culture. At that point it was a new hardcover, and it was $6.95. That book was an argument for carrying hardcovers, and for me what it definitely enshrined was generosity and conversation. She did not need to do that. I'm just a person at the cash register while she's waiting for someone else to show up. It was a very brief conversation. Our three Random House reps were:

Charles Spaulding, who was African American, Ron Smith, who was Chicano, Maggie, a woman of color. And it was Ron who set up my first trip to New York.

First trip on business? I'm assuming you had been before.

No, that was my first New York trip ever.

Wow!

Yes, exactly. We hadn't found an understanding of what the potential for City Lights was yet. Ron had just come out of mass markets. There was a hierarchy in those days. You started in mass and then moved to trades and up. And with the whole industry being as hard as it was for people of color, I was really fortunate. He was fresh. He didn't have any baggage with us like other reps did because we were such a bad account then. But he understood what we were trying to do, because I was always asking about how this book got to me, who acquired it. It's important to have some idea of what the editor does, whether you are a buyer or a bookseller.

Ron Smith decided, *Let's send this kid to New York.* **So how did that go?**

In Ron's first season out, Vintage Contemporaries happened, Avventura happened, Pantheon Moderns happened. All these incredible paperbacks. Random House had always had a good backlist—Cather, Faulkner—but they were always doing backlist titles in mass market. All these three lists I just named, all of which came out in a relatively short period of two or three buying seasons, put a stamp on what we now consider a trade paperback format. So Vintage Contemporaries was Gary Fisketjon, Avventura was Erroll McDonald, Pantheon was André Schiffrin. And all were distinctively designed. It was really an amazing time.

I met Erroll, Gary, all the Pantheon folks, for the first time, and all became long relationships. Editors are typically excited to meet the people who sell their books. As booksellers we get immediate face-to-face feedback from customers who are excited that they found such and such book in our store. Authors, too, they get that immediate feedback at events. Editors not so much, so when a bookseller comes to the office and says, "I really loved this," it can be hugely exciting for them.

Ron had set this all up. He'd said, "Here's this kid who's buying for City Lights." And the benefit was, whatever economic situation we were in, the store's name was known. They might have been thinking, *Who the fuck is Paul Yamazaki?* But it meant something to say, "Here's the buyer from City Lights." And luckily for me, editors were not aware of the accounting side of it. They had no idea what distress we were in then!

How did you find the city?

It was such a positive experience. I was so fortunate. New York was different then. I was in the West Village and had a meeting at Random House in twelve minutes. I jumped in a cab and I gave the address. The cab driver immediately said, "Oh, Random House!" And he tried to pitch me a book. It blew my mind to give him just an address and he could say, "Oh, Random House!" I told him I was a little bit late, and he got me there in time.

Speaking of cabs, we're all drunk on whiskey now and should probably call it a night.

Part IV:
Breakfast

Good morning! By the sober light of day, let's wrap up with your thoughts about the future of the industry. Why do bookstores matter?

We are about the process of discovery. There has never been a year where there hasn't been something that has threatened our existence as an industry or made life as booksellers challenging. Some of the most exciting and dynamic bookstores are no longer with us. I'm thinking of Midnight Special in Los Angeles, St. Mark's Bookshop in New York, Hungry Mind in St. Paul, Minnesota, and Cody's Books in Berkeley. Not to be able to go to those stores any longer, at least in my topography, makes the world much smaller.

Three Lives in the West Village of New York City and Green Arcade in the Hub neighborhood of San Francisco were the two jewel-box bookstores that bracket the continent. They were both wonderfully expansive and deep—Three Lives still is!—despite what many of us would think of as confining spaces of 600 to 800 square feet. Patrick Marks, the founder of Green Arcade, shut the doors for good when he retired in 2023. Here's hoping Toby Cox can keep his brilliant, bustling West Village store from meeting the same fate.

And yet we've also seen a lot of stores open in recent years.

Yes! To see Word Up or Mahogany—or the changes at Point Reyes or East Bay—those are amazing stores and give me hope. Any time I walk into a store that has relatively new leadership I feel *delight*. Each store has its particular environment. And it's hard to articulate. The world disappears except for those 800 square feet. Each store has its own way of embracing you, embracing the reader, and creating a sense of the universe expanding. For anybody curious and interested in printed matter, the more bookstores you go into, the more you'll realize how many different ways there are to be curious. That helps us set a foundation to be more knowledgeable about the world we inhabit. Both the practical and the sheer joy of it.

What's an example?

Powell's in Chicago—I think it's generous to say that it's not organized the way most of us would think of organization. But there are so many interesting books in there. If you have time to rummage through, you'll find things that you simply couldn't find anyplace else. Last time I was there I found a biography of the daring French publisher Maurice Girodias. I hadn't even known such a book existed! At a great store you can look at twelve well-selected, serendipitous linear inches and find a universe. Each page of a book that broadens our horizons feels both daunting and wondrous.

We're in a moment where the acquisition of books has become much more global, both with where editors can be and where writers are from, but it does feel like New York is still the nexus.

I think it's really important, still, in the sense of giving a platform to editors from a wide variety of backgrounds to work together, and to be in one place for us to meet. And I hope we can maintain this great tradition. It's important to me to maintain the connection that we've worked over long periods of time to foster between editors and booksellers and between publishers and booksellers.

It is interesting because it does feel like the reading public, even a very well-informed reader, doesn't know about the relationship between editor and bookseller. They don't tend to know an editor's name, unless maybe they're Bob Gottlieb, and even then, it's a maybe. But that relationship informs their buying decisions

so much of the time. And we sometimes hear a dismissal of the "big five" publishers.

Yes, and to do so is to ignore the fact that books which so many of us have really enjoyed reading as *readers*, before we were booksellers, came from those houses. There are a lot of issues about conglomeration within the industry that I'm highly critical of. A lot of us share that criticism. But to me that's a separate thing. It's separate from looking at particular editors and the books they do, which for me, as an individual buyer at City Lights, having that level of conversation with them and knowledge makes me a much better buyer. One of the weaknesses of independent bookselling is that we tend to be relatively homogenous in our class background. And because these are our friends and colleagues, we know they are lovely people. But there tends to be some reductiveness, a lack of critical awareness. It's one of the things that City Lights has done, and that I have done specifically, which is to be really aware of class and race. And to factor that into curatorial and business decisions.

You see so many galleys come to you from every publishing house. Yet, there's been a similar volume of books being published as there was twenty, thirty, forty years ago.

The major difference between then and now is that the level of representation is much more specific. Having a list of a hundred titles was a lot in those days. Now the lists are larger, and we can have many more types of books all in one rep's bag. Since the pandemic we've still been down about 20 % in terms of the numbers of titles we carry. But what we've been doing is intentional, really deep backlist buys. There's no substitute for actually going through all the reports line by line, even if it's tens of thousands. Things we haven't stocked in fifteen years sometimes sell in the first two or three weeks back in store.

And it's not something you can approach in terms of, *Oh, what would the sales have been if we had always had it?* **Because if your store is too cluttered, then it's not browsable.**

It doesn't matter whether you're 60,000 square feet or less than a thousand. We all have space issues. It's not possible to carry everything. How you rotate is the interesting thing. At least for City Lights, this is where trust comes in. We've brought in stuff we haven't carried for 15 years—university press nonfiction—and it sells. But there are things, like Ann Quin for example, where the original Dalkey editions did not sell. The And Other Stories editions are doing really astoundingly well. If we had just looked at what the Dalkey sales records were, we would not have seen what could happen. So, yes, it's good to look at data, but there are so many kinds of unknowns.

Beyond word of mouth, social media and the internet have made backlist much more discoverable.

Yes, for example, somebody out there is clearly talking about Victor LaValle. And you know I've been championing his books for decades now. Of Victor's five books, collectively, I've been able to sell maybe 10 to

12 copies annually—and now that the book has been adapted for television, we're selling 6 a week. I'm proud to have kept Victor's books on the shelves all along.

There's so much good stuff coming out every week, it's hard to decide what to face out on the display.

Yes, it's hard to keep things. It's hard to let stuff grow those legs. But it can be really gratifying to see something grow. Some of it is just inexplicable, though, where something didn't move at all on the display, but as soon as you put it back in section, it starts popping and there's just no explanation that you can find for it. Someone just told me that the reason we've been selling the shit out of *Carmilla*, the J. Sheridan Le Fanu vampire book, was that it had blown up on TikTok. Something that's hard is when the publisher runs out of stock on a book like that and, by the time it's back in stock, people have moved on.

Especially with literary publishing becoming more adventurous! I think that's your role as the head buyer of a store: to find who is willing to read outside of their box.

As booksellers we really have to get out of our own, what I'll politely call, middle-class white regressivism—not progressivism. We've used that framework as an economic tool for why we carry certain things and not others. The larger issue for all of us is how we get the understanding of our staff up to speed. Our staffs are a great resource and hold potential for education. It's not just their enthusiasm, but actually the ability to foster a tempered enthusiasm, in acknowledging that we're still a business while also acknowledging that there's a lot of ability to branch out into broader categories of reading.

You shouldn't disrespect where people come from as readers if they're primarily reading in a genre. But part of our job as independent booksellers is to look at categories. Given what we know about the structures of corporate publishing, a lot of the people who make those types of decisions about how a book is categorized have relatively little experience, and have even less experience with independents. So, to me, it's almost a waste of time to critique corporate publishing for this too much. This is our job: to translate, and even define, what a book is.

What do you say to booksellers who feel they're undervalued or underpaid?

We made the choice to be booksellers with an understanding of how the business works and what that means for us economically. We could have made other decisions. It's personally immensely gratifying, which isn't to say that we haven't put up with too much, asked for too little. We can no longer perpetuate this issue.

What we have to do now is to be able to look at all these various models of bookselling and make it slightly less economic suicide for others to make that same decision. For me, the task is how to bring in booksellers we know who are doing really radical things, really worthy things, and how do we give them a better understanding of how that fits into the realistic structures of the business. We don't want them to lose any of their radicalism, though!

How do you preserve that?

By figuring out where your maximum energy is best applied. It doesn't mean dissuading effort—not, *Oh, your energy is wasted here*—but it's more about being canny about where to apply your max effort. As a person who's working on weightlifting, it's figuring out where is it worth my literal bodily energy and bodily strength to apply max effort, and where is it worth it to use what's called a "rate of perceived exertion" of 7 or 8 out of 10. Contrary to what a lot of people probably think about exercising and weightlifting, most of the time you actually want to be at 7 or 8. You don't want to be at 10 all the time because then you're at failure. And it's trying to figure out where to apply that high exertion. For people of color, especially working in systems that aren't designed for them and have been designed to keep them out of bookstores and publishing, you don't want to be expending full effort at fixing everything at all times, because you will burn out.

There's that old communist slogan "from each according to his ability, to each according to his need," that I feel somehow got lost in translation on both sides: the population that is against anything that looks like a handout, and then frustrated middle-class progressives who want to see the results of the work but don't want to put in the work. There's a mismatch of who has the ability and who has the need. But I don't really know how to fix that in the bookselling context. I don't know if there is a fix. I think it's why I continue to have my so-called generosity, which is really more curiosity about what different people do and why.

A lot of my generosity comes from being raised a certain way. Being Asian American, being a person of color—not just in the publishing business, but coming from a specific background—you have to negotiate a lot of spaces, and I had guidance to become good at that, especially navigating very different camps to work together for an effective outcome.

Not quite code switching, but almost like reading the room.

Yes, reading the room, and I'm also genuinely curious about what other booksellers are thinking. It's not just politics, it's genuine enjoyment and coming with the perspective of trying to shape this business in a way that works for all of us.

"When a bookstore closes, an argument ends," wrote Adam Gopnik. What exciting conversations aren't happening anymore because of bookstore closures?

Not to have Cody's, for example, we've lost the ability to browse books from obscure places that most bookstores and readers don't have access to. Each bookstore has its own particular kind of magic. If that disappears... Yes, there are other bookstores, but it's not *that* bookstore. Each bookstore that succeeds in its mission creates an individual stamp. The fact that City Lights succeeds in that goal speaks well of our colleagues. What's inspiring is this new cohort of booksellers. This generation of booksellers has a level of foresight and knowledge in a way that my generation did not. We had the passion, but we were like sightless people walking down a dark corridor. Some of us found the light but weren't sure how. The institutions that support these new stores, like the ABA and regional associations, deserve credit for it.

Do you have regrets?

As I get older, I get slower, and there are more books coming and more books stacking up. I've made plenty of mistakes. To me, it is really interesting to make something that may have been written many years ago relevant to a situation that I might find myself in, and so I've been guilty of egregious textual fundamentalism. I've taken texts out of historical context and not taken into account how and where and when it was created. In contemporary America what distresses me a lot, no matter what the ideological perspective, I see so little historical awareness of when a work was created, which makes me think of how religious texts are interpreted. Karen Armstrong's *The Lost Art of Scripture* and David Blight's *Race and Reunion* helped me understand how ideas are dehistoricized and made into ideological instruments.

In considering that City Lights has just marked its 70th anniversary, then, how do you make a store like City Lights sustainable for the long-term?

Leaning into what makes us unique. Making title selections that are not always about demand but that consider what sells and what doesn't. The ABA has provided us with the analytical tools so that we can create empirical spreadsheet models. If we take x and do this over y period of time, what would the impact of that be?

You're known as a mentor and inspiration to younger people in the industry.

The generosity I have with young people comes from the way I am with my family. There couldn't be more intense disagreements than what I would have with my uncles and grandparents, and yet they were generous with me. They had opposing views, but I now realize that I put them at a certain social disadvantage. The thing that is heartening to me is that these young booksellers seem to have no second thoughts about hierarchies. If there's an issue, they'll address it. They'll pick up the phone and call anyone. They won't stand on ceremony.

What to you constitutes a meaningful life?

The point of justice, to me, is that everyone has an equal shot at joy, but joy is much more than just being so-called "happy." Joy is the enhancement of happiness through knowledge. We as booksellers have more of an opportunity to spread that joy through the books we present and those we find meaningful. Books are still, in my mind, one of the great technologies. For the transference of imagination, there is nothing better, to my mind. For the broad expanse of sharing and the interplay of imagination, it's hard for me to think what could be better. The length and breadth of the possibilities of joy are extended by the more we know and the more able we are to make our own informed decisions. Books become the fulcrum of conversation. The books by themselves could get you there as an individual but. for most of us, the dialogue back and forth increases the possibility of joy. I think that's the point of being a bookseller and the point of reading—and, really, the point of life.

Acknowledgments

In my five decades as a bookseller, there have been so many from the community of books who have been generous with their time and knowledge, and, without their patience and wisdom, the pages of this book would have been blank. I am grateful to my City Lights colleagues past and present: Lawrence Ferlinghetti, Shig Murao, Nancy Peters, Francis Oka, Elaine Katzenberger, Andy Bellows, Stacey Lewis, and Peter Maravelis have been comrades in the project we call City Lights.

I am indebted to the following for their counsel and comradeship, without which there would be no stories to tell: Nick Setka, Richard Bray, Bob Contant, Gary Thorpe, Roger Moss, Ron Smith, Oliver Gilliland, Richard Howorth, Mitchell Kaplan, Laurel Schreck, Barney Rosset, Drenka Willen, Ted Wilentz, Sonny Mehta, Morgan Entrekin, Barbara Epler, Dawn Davis, Ruth Liebmann, Erroll McDonald, Jim Sitter, Fiona McCrae, Mieke Chew, Judy Hottensen, Sarah McNally, Sean McDonald, Ira Silverberg, Laurie Callahan, Elisabeth Schmitz, Veronica Liu, Hannah Oliver Depp.

City Lights from its earliest days has had a special relationship to New Directions and Grove. I have particularly benefited as a bookseller and reader with both these presses.

Conversations with Stephen Sparks, Melinda Powers, and Vanessa Martini were essential to the ruminations in this book. Rick Simonson is, in fact, the co-author of this book and has very generously provided the foreword. Many of the thoughts and stories here originate with the long walks and conversations that I've had with Rick over the decades. Jeff Deutsch has been a wonderful collaborator and work